STEP-BY-STEP

THAI
COOKERY

GREENWICH EDITIONS

Specially produced for Greenwich Editions
Unit 7, 202-208 New North Road
London, N1 7BJ

© Salamander Books Ltd., 1995

ISBN 0 862 880 319

Author: Hilaire Walden
Photographer: David Gill

Printed and bound in Slovenia

OTHER TITLES IN THIS SERIES:

CONTENTS

INTRODUCTION

Thai food is an original and rich amalgam of evocative aromas, subtle blends of herbs and spices and contrasting textures and tastes. It contains flavours and techniques that are familiar from Chinese, Indian and Japanese cooking, but they have been so skilfully combined and refined that the resulting dishes have a new and exciting character.

The dishes are light and fresh. Vegetables are important, and are quickly cooked to retain their crispness, flavour and nutrients. Dairy products are not used and fish and poultry feature more prominently than meat; and where this is used it often only constitutes a small portion of the dish.

Equipment is minimal and simple, and the basic preparation of the food and its cooking is straightforward. Thai dishes are cooked quickly, with many taking only a few minutes, and the majority no more than 8-12 minutes. This factor, coupled with the informal way in which the dishes can be served and eaten, everyone helping themselves, makes a Thai meal ideal for today's style of casual entertaining.

Although traditionally all the dishes are served at once, Thai food is so adaptable that there is no problem in dividing it into Western-style courses. Many of the dishes can also be served as snacks or simple one-dish meals.

THE TASTE OF THAI

The flavours that characterize Thai food are the citrus-limes, spiked with clean pine notes, fresh coriander, coconut milk, garlic and chillies. A fresh sweet-sour taste is also typically Thai, derived from tangy lime or tamarind and palm sugar. Mild fish sauce provides the main savoury flavouring.

Rice is a very important part of the diet. As well as being the foundation of many one course dishes rice plays a vital supporting role for other dishes, and dilutes highly spiced ones. A point worth remembering when eating Thai food is that dishes are created specifically to be mixed and eaten with rice.

Thai curries are a case in point, as they can be searingly hot. Unlike Indian curries, Thai curries are cooked quickly and do not have the rich heaviness that results from long, slow simmering. Coconut milk is used to soften the pungency of the spices and combines flavours to give a sophisticated subtlety to the finished dish.

Thailand has a long coastline and many inland rivers, which provide fish and shellfish which are both ubiquitous and varied. Freshwater and sea fish are frequently cooked whole with the head and tail intact, having been cleaned beforehand.

Meat is considered more of a luxury and is often 'stretched' by combining with vegetables, rice, noodles, fish or shellfish or plenty of coconut based sauce. Chicken is more abundant, but the birds are smaller than Western farm reared ones. Duck is popular, particularly for special occasions. Many vegetables are used but they are not often cooked on their own or served as a specific dish. Instead they are combined with meat, poultry or fish, and eaten as a salad, either hot or cold, or simply served with 'Nam prik' (see page 16). The appearance of food matters to the Thais, and they like to add beautifully sculptured garnishes of fruit or vegetables to the finished dishes.

EATING THAI FOOD

Thais eat about 450 g (1 lb/3 cups) of rice a day. They might start with a rice soup, perhaps spooned over an egg, or simple fried rice. Lunch will be a composite rice or noodle soup, followed by crisp-fried noodles tossed with a little fish or meat, vegetables or flavourings.

The main meal is eaten in the evening, preferably in the company of an extended family and several friends. Traditionally, Thais will eat sitting on plump cushions set around a low table. All dishes are served simultaneously, rather than as separate courses, and everyone shares them.

Surrounding the large central bowl of rice there will be several dishes giving a balanced selection of flavours and textures. Usually they will consist of a soft steamed dish contrasted by a crisp fried one; one that is strongly flavoured (usually 'fired' by chillies), matched by a bland one. There are

cool, crunchy salads, bowls of sauces, plus a small bowl of clear soup for each diner.

There is no structure to the meal. Every diner dips into any dish they choose, putting a portion on their plate to mix with rice. The helpings are always small, but several helpings may be taken from each dish. An ordinary family meal ends with an array of fresh tropical fruits: mangosteens, rambutans, mangoes, papayas and lychees; all neatly sliced and arranged for everyone to share. Desserts only appear on special occasions or at formal banquets.

Thais like to eat little and often so throughout the day they will buy ready made sweets, cakes and savoury snacks from the numerous street vendors. Some of these savoury snacks such as Pork & Noodle Parcels (page 29) and Stuffed Eggs (page 27) could be served as a Western style first course.

—COOKING AND EQUIPMENT—

The majority of Thai cooking is done in one piece of cooking equipment, the wok, by either of two very straightforward cooking methods, steaming or stir-frying. Stir-frying is a very rapid process as the ingredients are cut into small, even pieces. For successful stir-frying, heat the wok before adding the oil to help prevent food from sticking, then heat the oil until it is almost smoking before adding the ingredients. Toss the food during cooking, and keep it moving from the centre of the wok to the sides. Because of its curved shape, the wok allows the food to be quickly tossed without spilling. As the food is kept moving during stir-frying, very little oil is needed.

1 wok with small bamboo steamer and rack; 2 bamboo handled wire basket; 3 spatula; 4 pestle and mortar; 5 cleaver.

Equipment

The amount of equipment needed for Thai cooking is minimal. Moreover, it is possible to prepare and cook Thai food using equipment that is readily to hand in most Western kitchens, but even authentic equipment is now familiar and readily available due to the popularity of Chinese cooking.

Wok – used for frying, stir-frying, deep-frying and steaming. A useful size to buy is about 30-35 cm (12-14 in) in diameter across the top. Choose one that has good deep sides and some weight. Carbon steel is preferable to light stainless steel or aluminium as these tend to develop hot spots which cause sticking, and do not withstand intense heat so well. Non-stick woks and electric ones do not reach sufficiently high temperatures.

A frying pan could be used for frying and stir-frying, a deep-fat frying pan for deep frying and a saucepan for steaming.

Wok stand – metal ring or stand to hold wok steady over the heat.

Rack – for using in a wok when steaming to support the steaming basket or container of food above the level of the water.

Steamer – Chinese-style bamboo steamers are used in Thailand, but Western metal ones will do just as well.

Rice cooker – because of the amount of rice Thais eat and the number of people cooked for, many households now use an electric rice cooker. A heavy saucepan with a tight-fitting lid will be adequate for Western needs.

Pestle and mortar – Used during the preparation of the majority of savoury dishes. A small blender or a coffee grinder kept specifically for the purpose will take away the effort but will not produce quite the same results. When used for fibrous ingredients such as galangal and lemon grass, the pestle and mortar crushes the fibres rather than cuts them and so releases the flavouring juices and oils more successfully.

Knives – Thais use cleavers, but a selection of sizes of good quality sharp knives will suffice.

Spatula – a long handled spatula that is curved and shaped like a shovel for scooping and tossing food in the wok.

Almost without exception, Thai kitchens have a set of bamboo-handled wire baskets so they can quickly and easily plunge noodles into boiling water for the requisite short cooking time, and then speedily lift them out; different baskets are used for different types of noodles.

INGREDIENTS

Although some of the foods, principally vegetables, that are available in Thailand cannot be found in the West, a sufficiently wide range of ingredients can be obtained to produce authentic Thai dishes. All of the ingredients used in this book can be found without difficulty in Oriental and Indian stores, and are becoming increasingly available in good food shops and supermarkets.

Suitable alternatives have been mentioned where possible, although they may change the flavour of a recipe.

Banana leaves – used to make containers for steamed foods, to which they impart a delicate taste.

Basil leaves – Thai basil leaves, also called 'holy' basil, are darker and their flavour slightly deeper, less 'fresh' than ordinary sweet basil. Bundles of leaves can be frozen whole in a polythene bag for up to about 2 weeks; remove leaves as required and add straight to dishes. Substitute Thai sweet basil or ordinary sweet basil, if necessary.

Chillies – add flavour as well as 'hotness'. Thais favour small and very fiery 'bird's eye' chillies but elsewhere these are only available in specialist shops. Chillies are rarely labelled with the variety or an indication of 'hotness' so, as a rule of thumb, smaller varieties are invariably hotter than large ones. Dried chillies have a more earthy, fruity flavour.

The seeds and white veins inside a chilli are not only hotter than the flesh, but have less flavour, and are generally removed before using. Chillies contain an oil that can make the eyes and even the skin sting, so wash your hands after preparing them and avoid touching the eyes or mouth.

To be really safe, wear rubber gloves when handling chillies.

Chinese black mushrooms – these dried mushrooms have quite a pronounced flavour and must be soaked for 20-30 minutes before use. The stalks tend to be tough so are usually discarded. Available in Oriental food stores.

Coconut cream – the layer that forms on the top of coconut milk.

Coconut milk – not the liquid from inside a coconut, but extracted from shredded coconut flesh that has been soaked in water. Soak the shredded flesh of 1 medium coconut in 315 ml (10 fl oz/1¼ cups) boiling water for 30 minutes. Tip into a sieve lined with muslin or fine cotton and squeeze the cloth hard to extract as much liquid as possible. Coconut milk can also be made from unsweetened desiccated coconut soaked in boiling water, or milk which will be richer. Allow 315 ml (10 fl oz/1¼ cups) liquid to 225 g (8 oz/2⅔ cups) desiccated coconut. Put into a blender and mix for 1 minute. Refrigerate coconut milk.

Ready prepared coconut milk is sold canned (which affects the flavour slightly) and in plastic pouches.

Coriander leaves – best bought in large bunches rather than small packets. Stand whole bunches in cold water in a cool place.

Coriander roots – roots have a more muted taste than the leaves. Large coriander bunches sold in Middle Eastern stores often include the roots. Fresh roots will last for several days if kept wrapped in a cool place, or can be frozen. If unavailable, use coriander stalks.

Fish sauce (nam pla) – a clear brown liquid, rich in protein and B vitamins,

1 *galangal;* 2 *ginger;* 3 *coriander;* 4 *Chinese black mushrooms;* 5 *chillies;* 6 *Thai sweet basil;* 7 *Thai holy basil.*

that is the essential Thai seasoning. It is salty but the flavour is mild.

Galangal (galangale, laos, lengk haus) – there are two varieties, lesser and greater. The latter is preferred and more likely to be found in the West. It looks similar to root ginger but the skin is thinner, paler, more transluscent and tinged with pink. Its flavour is also similar to ginger but less hot and with definite seductive citrus, pine notes. To use, peel and thinly slice or chop. The whole root will keep for up to 2 weeks if wrapped in paper and kept in the cool drawer of the refrigerator. Or it can be frozen. Allow to thaw just sufficiently to enable the amount required to be sliced off, then return the root to the freezer. Galangal is also sold dried as a powder or slices; the latter giving the better flavour. Substitute 1 dried slice or 1 teaspoon powder to each 1 cm (½ in) used in a recipe; in recipes where fresh galangal is pounded with other spices, mix the dried form in after the pounding; elsewhere, use as normal.

Alternatively, use fresh root ginger.

Ginger (fresh root) – When buying fresh root ginger, choose firm, heavy pieces that have a slight sheen. They can be kept in a cool place for up to a week, but for longer storage, wrap in absorbent kitchen paper, place in a polythene bag and store in the salad drawer of the refrigerator.

Kaffir limes – slightly smaller than ordinary limes with dark green, knobby rind. The smell and taste of the peel resemble aromatic lime with hints of lemon. The peel of ordinary limes can be substituted.

Kaffir lime leaves – the smooth, dark green leaves give an aromatic, clean citrus-pine flavour and smell. They keep well in a cool place and can be frozen.

Use ordinary lime peel if kaffir lime leaves are unavailable, substituting 1½ teaspoons finely grated peel for 1 kaffir lime leaf.

Lemon grass – a long, slim bulb with a lemon-citrus flavour. To use, cut off the root tip, peel off the tough outer layers and cut away the top part of stalk. The stalks will keep for several days in a cool place, or they can be chopped and frozen. If unavailable, use the grated rind of ½ lemon in place of 1 stalk.

Long beans – although these can grow to over 1 metre (3 feet) it is best to use younger ones. Green beans or French beans can replace them.

Mint – Thai mint has a spearmint flavour. If not available, Western spearmint or garden mint are the best substitutes.

Noodles – most types are interchangeable but two, rice stick noodles and mung bean noodles, can be crisp-fried. Dried noodles are usually soaked in cold water for 10-20 minutes until softened, before cooking; in general, the weight will have doubled after soaking. After draining, the cooking will usually be brief.

Mung bean noodles (glass, shining, bean thread or cellophane noodles) – tough and semi-transparent raw, they are soaked in warm water before cooking, when they turn to a jelly-like texture.

Fresh rice noodles packaged cooked and wet in wide, pliable 'hanks'. To use, without unwinding, cut into ribbons and stir into a dish just to warm through.

Rice stick noodles (rice vermicelli) – thin, brittle and semi-transluscent, they are sold in bundles. For most uses the noodles must be soaked before cooking, but when they are to be served crisp they are used dry.

Egg noodles – these thin wheat flour-based noodles are sold in both fresh (which do not need soaking) and dry 'nests'.

Palm sugar – brown sugar with a slight caramelized flavour. Sold in cakes. If unavailable use granulated sugar and demerara sugar in equal proportions.

Pandanus (screwpine) – both the leaves and the distilled essence of the flowers, called kewra water or essence, are used to give an exotic, musky, grassy flavour to sweet dishes.

Pea aubergine (eggplant) – very small aubergines (eggplants) about the size of a pea, and usually the same colour, although they can be white, purple or yellow. The fresh, slightly bitter taste is used raw in hot sauces and cooked in curries.

Rice – Thais mainly use a good quality variety of long-grain white rice called 'fragrant' rice. Ordinary long-grain white rice can be substituted. To cook, rinse the rice several times in cold running water. Put the rice into a heavy saucepan with 315 ml (10 fl oz/1¼ cups) water, cover and bring quickly to boil. Uncover and stir vigorously until the water has evaporated. Reduce the heat to very low, cover the pan tightly with foil, then place on the lid. Steam for 20 minutes until the rice is tender, light, fluffy and every grain is separate.

'Sticky' or 'glutinous' rice – an aptly-named short, round grain variety. It can be formed into balls and eaten with fingers, or used for desserts.

Ground browned rice – sometimes added to dishes to give texture; for this, dry-fry raw long-grain white rice until well-browned, then grind finely.

Shallots – Thai red shallots are smaller than Western shallots. They have quite a pronounced flavour that is almost fruity rather than pungent. Ordinary shallots can be substituted.

Shrimps, dried – whole dried shrimps are used to add texture and an attractive flavour.

Shrimp paste – a pungent, salty paste that is packed in jars, cans and plastic packets. It should be kept in a cool place.

Tamarind – sold in sticky brown-black blocks and provides a sharp, slightly fruity taste. To make tamarind water, break off a 25 g (1 oz) piece, pour over 315 ml (10 fl oz/1¼ cups) boiling water. Break up the lump with a spoon, then leave for about 30 minutes, stirring occasionally. Strain off the tamarind water, pressing on the pulp; discard the remaining debris. Keep the water in a jar in the refrigerator. Ready-to-use tamarind syrup can sometimes be bought; it is usually more concentrated, so less is used.

1 *pandanus leaf*; 2 *lemon grass*; 3 *kaffir lime leaves*; 4 *Thai mint*; 5 *palm sugar*; 6 *shallots*; 7 *dried shrimp*; 8 *pea aubergines (eggplants)*; 9 *long beans*.

GREEN CURRY PASTE

2 teaspoons coriander seeds
1 teaspoon cumin seeds
1 teaspoon black peppercorns
8 fresh green chillies, seeded and chopped
3 shallots, chopped
4 cloves garlic, crushed
3 coriander roots, chopped
2.5 cm (1 in) piece galangal, chopped
2 stalks lemon grass, chopped
2 kaffir lime leaves, chopped
2 teaspoons shrimp paste
2 tablespoons chopped coriander leaves

Heat a wok, add coriander and cumin seeds and heat until aroma rises.

Using a pestle and mortar or small blender, crush coriander and cumin seeds with peppercorns.

Add remaining ingredients and pound or mix to a smooth paste. Store in an airtight jar in the refrigerator for up to 4 weeks.

Makes about 8 tablespoons.

Note: The yield and hotness will vary according to the size and heat of the chillies.

RED CURRY PASTE

1 tablespoon coriander seeds
1 teaspoon cumin seeds
1 teaspoon black peppercorns
4 cloves garlic, chopped
3 coriander roots, chopped
8 dried red chillies, seeded and chopped
2 stalks lemon grass, chopped
grated peel ½ kaffir lime
3 cm (1 ¼ in) piece galangal, chopped
2 teaspoons shrimp paste

Heat a wok, add coriander and cumin seeds and heat until aroma rises. Using a pestle and mortar or small blender, crush coriander and cumin seeds with peppercorns.

Add remaining ingredients and pound or mix to a smooth paste. Store in an airtight jar in the refrigerator for up to 4 weeks.

Makes about 4 tablespoons.

Note: The yield and hotness will vary according to the size and heat of the chillies.

NAM PRIK

1 tablespoon fish sauce
about 22 whole dried shrimps, chopped
3 cloves garlic, chopped
4 dried red chillies with seeds, chopped
2 tablespoons lime juice
1 fresh red or green chilli, seeded and chopped
about 1 tablespoon pea aubergines (pea eggplants), if
    desired, chopped

Using a pestle and mortar or small blender, pound or mix fish sauce, shrimps, garlic, dried chillies and lime juice to a paste.

Stir in fresh red or green chilli and pea aubergines (pea eggplants), if desired. Transfer paste to a small bowl.

Serve with a selection of raw vegetables. Store in a covered jar in the refrigerator for several weeks.

Serves 6-8.

DIPPING SAUCE 1

8 tablespoons tamarind water, see page 13
½ - ¾ teaspoon crushed palm sugar
1 - 2 drops fish sauce
½ teaspoon very finely chopped spring onion (scallion)
½ teaspoon very finely chopped garlic
½ teaspoon finely chopped fresh red chilli

In a small saucepan, gently heat tamarind water and sugar until sugar has dissolved.

Remove pan from heat and add fish sauce. Stir in spring onion (scallion), garlic and chilli. Pour into a small serving bowl and leave to cool.

Serves 4.

DIPPING SAUCE 2

6 tablespoons lime juice
1 ½ - 2 teaspoons crushed palm sugar
½ teaspoon fish sauce
½ teaspoon very finely chopped red shallot
½ teaspoon very finely chopped fresh green chilli
½ teaspoon finely chopped fresh red chilli

In a small bowl, stir together lime juice and sugar until sugar has dissolved. Adjust amount of sugar, if desired.

Stir in fish sauce, shallot and chillies. Pour into a small serving bowl. Serve with deep-fried fish, fish fritters, won tons or spring rolls.

Serves 4.

LEMON GRASS SOUP

175-225 g (6-8 oz) raw large prawns
2 teaspoons vegetable oil
625 ml (20 fl oz/2½ cups) light fish stock
2 thick stalks lemon grass, finely chopped
3 tablespoons lime juice
1 tablespoon fish sauce
3 kaffir lime leaves, chopped
½ fresh red chilli, seeded and thinly sliced
½ fresh green chilli, seeded and thinly sliced
½ teaspoon crushed palm sugar
coriander leaves, to garnish

Peel prawns and remove dark veins running down their backs; reserve prawns.

In a wok, heat oil, add prawn shells and fry, stirring occasionally, until they change colour. Stir in stock, bring to boil and simmer for 20 minutes. Strain stock and return to wok; discard shells. Add lemon grass, lime juice, fish sauce, lime leaves, chillies and sugar. Simmer for 2 minutes.

Add prawns and cook just below simmering point for 2-3 minutes until prawns are cooked. Serve in warmed bowls garnished with coriander.

Serves 4.

VERMICELLI SOUP

1.1 litres (2 pints/5 cups) chicken stock
1 small onion, chopped
2 stalks lemon grass, chopped and crushed
2 kaffir lime leaves, shredded
1 tablespoon lime juice
3 cloves garlic, chopped
2 fresh red chillies, seeded and chopped
4 cm (1½ in) piece galangal, peeled and chopped
1½ tablespoons fish sauce
2 teaspoons crushed palm sugar
115 g (4 oz) clear vermicelli, soaked in cold water for
   10 minutes, drained
2 tablespoons roughly chopped coriander leaves
Thai holy basil leaves, to garnish

Put stock, onion, lemon grass, lime leaves, lime juice, garlic, chillies and galangal into a saucepan and simmer for 20 minutes.

Stir in fish sauce and sugar. When sugar has dissolved, add noodles and cook for 1 minute. Stir in coriander. Spoon into warmed bowls and garnish with basil leaves.

Serves 4-6.

–CHICKEN & MUSHROOM SOUP–

2 cloves garlic, crushed
4 coriander sprigs
1½ teaspoons black peppercorns, crushed
1 tablespoon vegetable oil
1 litre (35 fl oz/4¼ cups) chicken stock
5 pieces dried Chinese black mushrooms, soaked in
   cold water for 20 minutes, drained and coarsely
   chopped
1 tablespoon fish sauce
115 g (4 oz) chicken, cut into strips
55 g (2 oz) spring onions (scallions), thinly sliced
coriander sprigs, to garnish

Using a pestle and mortar or small blender,
pound or mix garlic, coriander stalks and
leaves and peppercorns to a paste. In a wok,
heat oil, add paste and cook, stirring, for 1
minute. Stir in stock, mushrooms and fish
sauce. Simmer for 5 minutes.

Add chicken, lower heat so liquid barely
moves and cook gently for 5 minutes. Scatter
spring onions (scallions) over surface and
garnish with coriander sprigs.

Serves 4.

PORK & PEANUT SOUP

4 coriander roots, chopped
2 cloves garlic, chopped
1 teaspoon black peppercorns, cracked
1 tablespoon vegetable oil
225 g (8 oz) lean pork, finely chopped
4 spring onions (scallions), chopped
700 ml (24 fl oz/3 cups) veal stock
55 g (2 oz) skinned peanuts
6 pieces dried Chinese black mushrooms, soaked for
    20 minutes, drained and chopped
115 g (4 oz) bamboo shoots, roughly chopped
1 tablespoon fish sauce

Using a pestle and mortar, pound coriander, garlic and peppercorns to a paste.

In a wok, heat oil, add peppercorn paste and cook for 2-3 minutes, stirring occasionally. Add pork and spring onions (scallions) and stir for 1½ minutes.

Stir stock, peanuts and mushrooms into wok, then cook at just below boiling point for 7 minutes. Add bamboo shoots and fish sauce and continue to cook gently for 3-4 minutes.

Serves 3-4.

— CHICKEN & COCONUT SOUP —

950 ml (30 fl oz / 3¾ cups) coconut milk
115 g (4 oz) chicken breast meat, cut into strips
2 stalks lemon grass, bruised and thickly sliced
2 spring onions (scallions), thinly sliced
3-4 fresh red chillies, seeded and sliced
juice 1½ limes
1 tablespoon fish sauce
1 tablespoon coriander leaves, freshly torn into shreds
coriander leaves, to garnish

Bring coconut milk to just below boiling point in a saucepan. Add chicken and lemon grass.

Adjust heat so liquid gives just an occasional bubble, then poach chicken, uncovered, for about 4 minutes until tender.

Add spring onions (scallions) and chillies. Heat briefly, then remove from heat and stir in lime juice, fish sauce and shredded coriander. Serve garnished with coriander leaves.

Serves 4.

GOLD BAGS

115 g (4 oz) cooked peeled prawns, finely chopped
55 g (2 oz) canned water chestnuts, finely chopped
2 spring onions (scallions), white part only, finely chopped
1 teaspoon fish sauce
freshly ground black pepper
16 won ton skins
vegetable oil for deep frying
Dipping Sauce 1, see page 17
coriander sprig, to garnish

In a bowl, mix together prawns, water chestnuts, spring onions (scallions), fish sauce and black pepper.

To shape each bag, put a small amount of prawn mixture in centre of each won ton skin. Dampen edges of skins with a little water, then bring up over filling to form a 'dolly bag'. Press edges together to seal.

In a wok, heat oil to 190C (375F). Add bags in batches and fry for about 2-3 minutes until crisp and golden. Using a slotted spoon transfer to absorbent kitchen paper to drain. Serve hot with dipping sauce. Garnish with coriander sprig.

Makes 16.

SWEETCORN CAKES

350 g (12 oz) sweetcorn kernels
1 tablespoon Green Curry Paste, see page 14
2 tablespoons plain flour
3 tablespoons rice flour
3 spring onions (scallions), finely chopped
1 egg, beaten
2 teaspoons fish sauce
vegetable oil for deep frying
2.5 cm (1 in) piece cucumber
Dipping Sauce 2, see page 18
1 tablespoon ground roasted peanuts

Place sweetcorn in a blender, add curry paste, plain flour, rice flour, spring onions (scallions), egg and fish sauce and mix together so corn is slightly broken up. Form into about 16 cakes. Heat oil in a wok to 180C (350F), then deep fry one batch of sweetcorn cakes for about 3 minutes until golden brown.

Using a slotted spoon, transfer to absorbent kitchen paper to drain. Keep warm while frying remaining cakes. Peel cucumber, quarter lengthwise, remove seeds, then slice thinly. Place in a small bowl and mix in dipping sauce and ground peanuts. Serve with warm sweetcorn cakes.

Makes about 16.

STEAMED CRAB

1 clove garlic, chopped
1 small shallot, chopped
6 coriander sprigs, stalks finely chopped
175 g (6 oz) cooked crab meat
115 g (4 oz) lean pork, very finely chopped and cooked
1 egg, beaten
1 tablespoon coconut cream, see page 11
2 teaspoons fish sauce
freshly ground black pepper
1 fresh red chilli, seeded and cut into fine strips

Grease 4 individual heatproof dishes and place in a steaming basket.

Using a pestle and mortar, pound garlic, shallot and coriander stalks to a paste. In a bowl, stir together crab meat, pork, garlic paste, egg, coconut cream, fish sauce and plenty of black pepper until evenly mixed.

Divide between dishes, arrange coriander leaves and strip of chilli on tops. Place steaming basket over a saucepan of boiling water and steam for about 12 minutes until mixture is firm.

Serves 4.

Note: Crab shells may be used instead of dishes for cooking.

STUFFED EGGS

4 large eggs, at room temperature
4 tablespoons minced cooked pork
4 tablespoons finely chopped peeled prawns
1 teaspoon fish sauce
1 clove garlic, finely chopped
1½ tablespoons chopped coriander leaves
finely ground black pepper
lettuce leaves, to serve
coriander sprigs, to garnish

Form 4 'nests' from foil to hold eggs upright.
Place in a steaming basket. Cook eggs in pan
of gently boiling water for 1½ minutes;
remove.

Carefully peel a small part of pointed end of
eggs. With the point of a slim, sharp knife,
cut a small hole down through the exposed
white of each egg; reserve pieces of white that
are removed. Pour liquid egg yolk and white
from egg into a small bowl. Thoroughly mix
in pork, prawns, fish sauce, garlic, coriander
and pepper. Carefully spoon into eggs and
replace removed pieces of white.

Set steaming basket over a saucepan of
boiling water and place eggs, cut end upper-
most, in foil 'nests'. Cover basket and steam
eggs for about 12 minutes. When cool
enough to handle, carefully peel off shells.
Serve whole or halved on lettuce leaves,
garnished with coriander sprigs.

Serves 4.

PORK TOASTS

175 g (6 oz) lean pork, minced
55 g (2 oz) cooked peeled prawns, finely chopped
2 cloves garlic, finely chopped
1 tablespoon chopped coriander leaves
1½ spring onions (scallions), finely chopped
2 eggs, beaten
2 teaspoons fish sauce
freshly ground black pepper
4 day-old slices of bread
1 tablespoon coconut milk
vegetable oil for deep frying
coriander leaves, fine rings of fresh red chilli and
    cucumber slices, to garnish

In a bowl, mix together pork and prawns using a fork, then thoroughly mix in garlic, coriander, spring onions (scallions), half of egg, the fish sauce and black pepper. Divide between bread, spreading it firmly to edges. In a small bowl, stir together remaining egg and coconut milk and brush over pork mixture. Trim crusts from bread, then cut each slice into squares.

In a wok, heat oil to 190C (375F). Add several squares at a time, pork-side down, and fry for 3-4 minutes until crisp, turning over halfway through. Using a slotted spoon, transfer to absorbent kitchen paper to drain, then keep warm in oven. Check temperature of oil in between frying each batch. Serve warm, garnished with coriander and slices of chilli and cucumber.

Serves 4-6.

PORK & NOODLE PARCELS

3 cloves garlic, chopped
4 coriander roots, chopped
175 g (6 oz) lean pork, minced
1 small egg, beaten
2 teaspoons fish sauce
freshly ground black pepper
about 55 g (2 oz) egg thread noodles (1 'nest')
vegetable oil for deep frying
Dipping Sauce 1, see page 17, to serve
coriander sprig, to garnish

Using a pestle and mortar or small blender, pound or mix together garlic and coriander roots. In a bowl, mix together pork, egg, fish sauce and pepper, then stir in garlic mixture.

Place noodles in a heatproof sieve and dip in boiling water for 5 seconds if fresh, about 2 minutes if dried, until separated. Remove and rinse immediately in cold running water. Form pork mixture into approximately 12 balls. Neatly and evenly wind 3 or 4 strands of noodles around each ball to cover completely.

In a wok, heat oil to 180C (350F). Using a slotted spoon, lower 4-6 balls into oil and cook for about 3 minutes until golden and pork is cooked through. Using a slotted or draining spoon, transfer to absorbent kitchen paper to drain, Keep warm while cooking remaining balls. Serve hot with dipping sauce. Garnish with coriander sprig.

Makes about 12 parcels.

CRAB ROLLS

225 g (8 oz) cooked chicken, very finely chopped
115 g (4 oz) cooked crabmeat, flaked
4 spring onions (scallions), finely chopped
25 g (1 oz) beansprouts, finely chopped
1 small carrot, grated
2 teaspoons fish sauce
freshly ground black pepper
about 9 rice paper wrappers, each about 18 cm (7 in) in
    diameter
vegetable oil for deep frying
Thai holy basil leaves, Thai mint leaves and lettuce
    leaves, to serve
Dipping Sauce 1, see page 17

In a bowl, mix together chicken, crabmeat, spring onions (scallions), beansprouts, carrot, fish sauce and black pepper. Brush both sides of each wrapper liberally with water and set aside to soften. Cut each into 4 wedges. Place a small amount of filling near wide end of one wedge, fold end over filling, tuck in sides and roll up. Repeat with remaining wedges and filling.

In a wok, heat oil to 190C (375F). Fry rolls in batches for 2-3 minutes until crisp and golden. Drain on absorbent kitchen paper. Serve hot. To eat, sprinkle each roll with herbs, then wrap in a lettuce leaf and dip into dipping sauce.

Makes about 36.

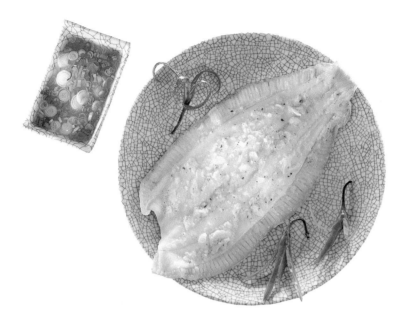

—CORIANDER FISH & GARLIC—

6 coriander roots, chopped
3 large cloves garlic, chopped
5 black peppercorns, crushed
2 fish fillets, such as trout or plaice
2 pieces banana leaf, if desired
3 tablespoons lime juice
1/2 teaspoon crushed palm sugar
1 spring onion (scallion), finely chopped
1/2 small fresh green chilli, seeded and thinly sliced
1/2 small fresh red chilli, seeded and thinly sliced

Using a pestle and mortar or small blender, briefly mix together coriander roots, garlic and peppercorns. Spread evenly over inside of fish fillets; set aside for 30 minutes.

Wrap fish in banana leaves or pieces of foil, securing leaf with wooden cocktail stick (toothpick), or folding edges of foil tightly together. Grill for about 8 minutes. Meanwhile, in a bowl, stir together lime juice and sugar, then stir in spring onion (scallion) and chillies. Serve with fish.

Serves 2.

FISH WITH GINGER

6 tablespoons vegetable oil
1 kg (2½ lb) whole white fish or single piece, such as
  cod, bass or red snapper
1 small onion, finely chopped
6 spring onions (scallions), thickly sliced
2 cloves garlic, crushed
1 tablespoon grated fresh root ginger
2 teaspoons fish sauce
1½ tablespoons light soy sauce
1 teaspoon crushed palm sugar
1 tablespoon tamarind water, see page 13
freshly ground black pepper
coriander sprigs, to garnish

Over a medium heat, heat 4 tablespoons oil in a wok. Add fish and fry for about 5 minutes a side until browned and flesh flakes easily when flaked with a knife. Meanwhile, heat remaining oil in a small saucepan over a moderate heat, add onion and cook, stirring occasionally, until browned. When fish is cooked, transfer to absorbent kitchen paper and keep warm.

Stir into wok, spring onions (scallions), garlic and ginger. Stir-fry for 2-3 minutes, then stir in fish sauce, soy sauce, palm sugar and tamarind water. Cook for 1 minute, season with black pepper, then pour over fish. Sprinkle over the browned onions and garnish with coriander.

Serves 4.

COCONUT FISH WITH GALANGAL

4 tablespoons vegetable oil
1 shallot, chopped
4 cm (1½ in) piece galangal, finely chopped
2 stalks lemon grass, finely chopped
1 small fresh red chilli, seeded and chopped
125 ml (4 fl oz/½ cup) coconut milk
2 teaspoons fish sauce
5 coriander sprigs
about 350 g (12 oz) white fish fillets, such as halibut,
    red snapper
1 small onion, sliced
freshly ground black pepper

In a wok, heat 1 tablespoon oil, add shallot, galangal, lemon grass and chilli. Stir for 3 minutes until lightly coloured. Transfer to a small blender, add coconut milk, fish sauce and stalks from coriander sprigs and process until well mixed. Place fish in a heatproof, shallow round dish that fits over a saucepan, and pour over spice sauce. Cover dish, place over pan of boiling water and steam for 8-10 minutes until flesh flakes.

Meanwhile, heat remaining oil in a wok over moderate heat, add onion and cook, stirring occasionally, until browned. Using a slotted spoon, transfer to absorbent kitchen paper. Add coriander leaves to oil and fry for a few seconds. Using a slotted spoon, transfer to absorbent kitchen paper to drain. Scatter fried onions and coriander over fish and grind over plenty of black pepper.

Serves 3-4.

PRAWNS WITH GARLIC

2 tablespoons vegetable oil
5 cloves garlic, chopped
0.5 cm (¼ in) slice fresh root ginger, very finely
 chopped
14-16 large prawns, peeled, tails left on
2 teaspoons fish sauce
2 tablespoons chopped coriander leaves
freshly ground black pepper
lettuce leaves, lime juice and diced cucumber, to serve

In a wok, heat oil, add garlic and fry until
browned.

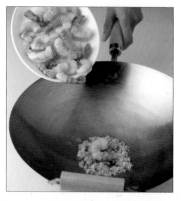

Stir in ginger, heat for 30 seconds, then add
prawns and stir-fry for 2-3 minutes until
beginning to turn opaque. Stir in fish sauce,
coriander, 1-2 tablespoons water and plenty
of black pepper. Allow to bubble for 1-2
minutes.

Serve prawns on a bed of lettuce leaves with
lime juice squeezed over and scattered with
cucumber.

Serves 4.

—PRAWNS IN COCONUT SAUCE—

2 fresh red chillies, seeded and chopped
1 red onion, chopped
1 thick stalk lemon grass, chopped
2.5 cm (1 in) piece galangal, chopped
1 teaspoon ground turmeric
250 ml (8 fl oz/1 cup) coconut milk
14-16 raw Mediterranean (king) prawns, peeled and
    deveined
8 Thai holy basil leaves
2 teaspoons lime juice
1 teaspoon fish sauce
1 spring onion (scallion), including some green, cut
    into fine strips

Using a small blender, mix chillies, onion, lemon grass and galangal to a paste. Transfer to a wok and heat, stirring, for 2-3 minutes. Stir in turmeric and 125 ml (4 fl oz/½ cup) water, bring to the boil and simmer for 3-4 minutes until most of the water has evaporated.

Stir in coconut milk and prawns and cook gently, stirring occasionally, for about 4 minutes until prawns are just firm and pink. Stir in basil leaves, lime juice and fish sauce. Scatter over strips of spring onion (scallion).

Serves 4.

JACKETED PRAWNS

4 cm (1½ in) length cucumber
Dipping Sauce 1, see page 17
8 raw Mediterranean (king) prawns
vegetable oil for deep frying
leaves from 1 coriander sprig, chopped
BATTER:
115 g (4 oz/⅔ cup) rice flour
3 tablespoons desiccated coconut
1 egg, separated
185 ml (6 fl oz/¾ cup) coconut milk
1 teaspoon fish sauce

Cut cucumber into quarters lengthwise, remove and discard seeds, then thickly slice. Place in a small bowl and add dipping sauce. Set aside. Peel prawns, leaving tails on. Cut along back of each one and remove black spinal cord. Set prawns aside. In a wok, heat oil to 180C (350F).

For batter, in a bowl, stir together flour and coconut. Gradually stir in egg yolk, coconut milk and fish sauce. In a bowl, whisk egg white until stiff; fold into batter. Dip prawns in batter to coat evenly. Deep fry in batches for 2-3 minutes until golden. Using a slotted spoon, transfer to absorbent kitchen paper. Keep warm while frying remainder. Add coriander to sauce and serve with prawns.

Serves 3-4.

SCALLOPS WITH LIME

12 scallops on the half shell
1 tablespoon vegetable oil
2 cloves garlic, chopped
1 red shallot, finely chopped
0.5 cm (¼ in) slice galangal, finely chopped
freshly ground black pepper
1 teaspoon finely chopped fresh red chilli
3 tablespoons lime juice
¼ teaspoon crushed palm sugar
1 teaspoon fish sauce
shredded coriander leaves, to garnish

Lay scallops on their shells in a steaming basket.

In a wok, heat oil, add garlic and shallot and cook, stirring occasionally, until softened. Add galangal and stir for 1 minute. Sprinkle over scallops and grind over black pepper. Cover steaming basket and place over a wok or saucepan of boiling water. Steam for 6-8 minutes until scallops just begin to turn opaque.

In a saucepan, gently heat chilli, lime juice, sugar and fish sauce until sugar dissolves. Transfer scallops on their shells to a warmed serving plate, spoon over lime sauce and scatter with coriander.

Serves 3-4.

— PRAWN & CUCUMBER CURRY —

4 tablespoons coconut cream, see page 11
3-4 tablespoons Red Curry paste, see page 15
225 g (8 oz) raw large peeled prawns
20 cm (8 in) length cucumber, halved lengthwise,
    seeded and cut into 2 cm (¾ in) pieces
315 ml (10 fl oz/1¼ cups) coconut milk
2 tablespoons tamarind water, see page 13
1 teaspoon crushed palm sugar
coriander leaves, to garnish

In a wok, heat coconut cream, stirring, until it boils, thickens and oil begins to form. Add curry paste. Stir in prawns to coat, then stir in cucumber. Add coconut milk, tamarind water and sugar.

Cook gently for about 3-4 minutes until prawns are just cooked through. Transfer to warmed serving dish and garnish with coriander.

Serves 3.

MUSSELS WITH BASIL

700 g (1½ lb) fresh mussels in shell, cleaned, bearded
    and rinsed
1 large clove garlic, chopped
7.5 cm (3 in) piece galangal, thickly sliced
2 stalks lemon grass, chopped
10 Thai holy basil sprigs
1 tablespoon fish sauce
Thai holy basil leaves, to garnish
Dipping Sauce 2, see page 18, to serve

Place mussels, garlic, galangal, lemon grass, basil sprigs and fish sauce in a large saucepan. Add water to a depth of 1 cm (½ in), cover pan, bring to the boil and cook for about 5 minutes, shaking pan frequently, until mussels have opened; discard any that remain closed.

Transfer mussels to a large warmed bowl, or individual bowls, and strain over cooking liquid. Scatter over basil leaves. Serve with sauce to dip mussels into.

Serves 2-3.

—CHICKEN IN COCONUT MILK—

8 black peppercorns, cracked
6 coriander roots, finely chopped
4.5 cm (1¾ in) piece galangal, thinly sliced
2 fresh green chillies, seeded and thinly sliced
625 ml (20 fl oz/2½ cups) coconut milk
grated peel 1 kaffir lime
4 kaffir lime leaves, shredded
1.35 kg (3 lb) chicken, cut into 8 pieces
1 tablespoon fish sauce
3 tablespoons lime juice
3 tablespoons chopped coriander leaves

Using a pestle and mortar or small blender, pound or mix together peppercorns, coriander roots and galangal.

In a wok, briefly heat peppercorn mixture, stirring, then stir in chillies, coconut milk, lime peel and leaves. Heat to just simmering point and add chicken portions. Adjust heat so liquid is barely moving, then cook gently for about 40-45 minutes until chicken is very tender and liquid reduced.

Stir in fish sauce and lime juice. Scatter coriander leaves over chicken and serve.

Serves 6-8.

BARBECUED CHICKEN

4 fresh red chillies, seeded and sliced
2 cloves garlic, chopped
5 shallots, finely sliced
2 teaspoons crushed palm sugar
125 ml (4 fl oz/½ cup) coconut cream, see page 11
2 teaspoons fish sauce
1 tablespoon tamarind water, see page 13
4 boneless chicken breasts
Thai holy basil leaves or coriander leaves, to garnish

Using a pestle and mortar or small blender, pound chillies, garlic and shallots to a paste. Work in sugar, then stir in coconut cream, fish sauce and tamarind water.

Using the point of a sharp knife, cut 4 slashes in chicken breast. Place chicken in a shallow dish and pour over spice mixture. Turn to coat, cover dish and set aside for 1 hour.

Preheat grill. Place chicken on a piece of foil and grill for about 4 minutes a side, basting occasionally, until cooked through. Garnish with basil or coriander leaves.

Serves 4.

LEMON GRASS CURRY CHICKEN

350 g (12 oz) boneless chicken, chopped into small
  pieces
1 tablespoon Red Curry Paste, see page 15
3 tablespoons vegetable oil
2 cloves garlic, finely chopped
1 tablespoon fish sauce
2 stalks lemon grass, finely chopped
5 kaffir lime leaves, shredded
½ teaspoon crushed palm sugar

Place chicken in a bowl, add curry paste and
stir to coat chicken; set aside for 30 minutes.

In a wok, heat oil, add garlic and fry until
golden. Stir in chicken, then fish sauce,
lemon grass, lime leaves, sugar and 125 ml
(4 fl oz/½ cup) water.

Adjust heat so liquid is barely moving and
cook for 15-20 minutes until chicken is
cooked through. If chicken becomes too dry,
add a little more water, but the final dish
should be quite dry.

Serves 3-4.

DUCK CURRY

5 tablespoons coconut cream, see page 11
5 tablespoons Green Curry Paste, see page 14
about 1.35 kg (3 lb) duck, skinned if desired, well-
    trimmed of excess fat, divided into 8 portions
625 ml (20 fl oz/2½ cups) coconut milk
1 tablespoon fish sauce
8 kaffir lime leaves, shredded
2 fresh green chillies, seeded and thinly sliced
12 Thai holy basil leaves
leaves from 5 coriander sprigs
coriander sprigs, to garnish

Heat coconut cream in a wok over a medium heat, stirring, until it thickens and oil begins to separate and bubble.

Stir in curry paste and cook for about 5 minutes until mixture darkens. Stir in duck pieces to coat with curry mixture. Lower heat, cover and cook for 15 minutes, stirring occasionally. If necessary, using a bulb baster, remove excess fat from the surface, or carefully spoon it off. Stir in coconut milk, fish sauce and lime leaves. Heat to just simmering point, then cook gently without boiling, turning duck over occasionally, for 30-40 minutes until meat is very tender. Remove surplus fat from surface, then stir in chillies.

Cook for a further 5 minutes. Stir in basil and coriander leaves and cook for a further 2 minutes. Garnish with coriander sprigs.

Serves 4.

–CHICKEN WITH MANGE TOUT–

3 tablespoons vegetable oil
3 cloves garlic, chopped
1 dried red chilli, seeded and chopped
3 red shallots, chopped
2 tablespoons lime juice
2 teaspoons fish sauce
350 g (12 oz) chicken, finely chopped
1½ stalks lemon grass, chopped
1 kaffir lime leaf, sliced
175 g (6 oz) mange tout (snow peas)
1½ tablespoons coarsely ground browned rice,
    see page 13
3 spring onions (scallions), chopped
chopped coriander leaves, to garnish

In a wok, heat 2 tablespoons oil, add garlic and cook, stirring occasionally, until lightly browned. Stir in chilli, shallots, lime juice, fish sauce and 4 tablespoons water. Simmer for 1-2 minutes, then stir in chicken, lemon grass and lime leaf. Cook, stirring, for 2-3 minutes until chicken is just cooked through. Transfer to a warmed plate and keep warm.

Heat remaining oil in wok, add mange tout (snow peas) and stir-fry for 2-3 minutes until just tender. Transfer to a warmed serving plate. Return chicken to wok. Add rice and spring onions (scallions). Heat for about 1 minute, then transfer to serving plate. Garnish with chopped coriander.

Serves 3-4.

BEEF CURRY

2 tablespoons vegetable oil
3 tablespoons Red Curry Paste, see page 15
350 g (12 oz) lean beef, cut into cubes
1 stalk lemon grass, finely chopped
115 g (4 oz) long beans, or green beans, cut into 4 cm
(1½ in) lengths
About 8 pieces dried Chinese black mushrooms,
smoked, drained and chopped
3 tablespoons roasted peanuts
1 fresh green chilli, seeded and chopped
1 tablespoon fish sauce
2 teaspoons crushed palm sugar
15 Thai mint leaves

In a wok, heat oil, add curry paste and stir for
3 minutes. Add beef and lemon grass and stir-
fry for 5 minutes. Add beans and mushrooms,
stir-fry for 3 minutes, then stir in peanuts and
chilli.

Stir for 1 minute, then stir in 4 tablespoons
water, the fish sauce and sugar and cook for
about 2 minutes until beans are tender but
crisp. Transfer to a warmed serving dish and
scatter over mint leaves.

Serves 3-4.

PORK SATAY

350 g (12 oz) lean pork, cubed
juice 1 lime
1 stalk lemon grass, finely chopped
1 clove garlic, chopped
2 tablespoons vegetable oil
SAUCE:
4 tablespoons vegetable oil
85 g (3 oz/½ cup) raw shelled peanuts
2 stalks lemon grass, chopped
2 fresh red chillies, seeded and sliced
3 shallots, chopped
2 cloves garlic, chopped
1 teaspoon fish paste
2 teaspoons crushed palm sugar
315 ml (10 fl oz/1¼ cups) coconut milk
juice ½ lime

Divide pork between 4 skewers and lay them in a shallow dish. In a bowl, mix together lime juice, lemon grass, garlic and oil. Pour over pork, turn to coat, cover and set aside in a cool place for 1 hour, turning occasionally.

Preheat grill. Remove pork from dish, allowing excess liquid to drain off. Grill, turning frequently and basting, for 8-10 minutes.

Meanwhile, make sauce. Over a high heat, heat 1 tablespoon oil in a wok, add nuts and cook, stirring constantly, for 2 minutes. Using a slotted spoon, transfer to absorbent kitchen paper to drain. Using a pestle and mortar or small blender, grind to a paste. Remove and set aside.

Using a pestle and mortar or small blender, pound or mix lemon grass, chillies, shallots, garlic and fish paste to a smooth paste.

Heat remaining oil in wok, add spice mixture and cook, stirring, for 2 minutes. Stir in peanut paste, sugar and coconut milk. Bring to boil, stirring, then adjust heat so sauce simmers. Add lime juice and simmer, stirring, for 5-10 minutes until thickened. Serve in a warmed bowl to accompany pork. Garnish with carrot flowers, see page 17, and lettuce leaves.

Serves 4.

— PORK & BAMBOO SHOOTS —

2 tablespoons vegetable oil
4 cloves garlic, very finely chopped
350 g (12 oz) lean pork, very finely chopped
115 g (4 oz) canned bamboo shoots, chopped or sliced
4 tablespoons peanuts, coarsely chopped
2 teaspoons fish sauce
freshly ground black pepper
4 large spring onions (scallions), thinly sliced
Thai holy basil sprig, to garnish

In a wok, heat oil, add garlic and fry, stirring occasionally, for about 3 minutes until lightly coloured.

Add pork and stir-fry for 2 minutes. Add bamboo shoots and continue to stir for a further minute.

Stir in peanuts, fish sauce, plenty of black pepper and half of spring onions (scallions). Transfer to a warmed serving plate and sprinkle over remaining spring onions (scallions) and basil sprig.

Serves 4.

— MIXED VEGETABLES & PORK —

225 g (8 oz) lean pork, finely chopped
freshly ground black pepper
2 tablespoons vegetable oil
3 cloves garlic, finely chopped
450 g (1 lb) prepared mixed vegetables, such as mange
    tout (snow peas), broccoli flowerets, red pepper
    (capsicum) and courgettes (zucchini)
1 tablespoon fish sauce
½ teaspoon crushed palm sugar
3 spring onions (scallions), finely chopped

In a bowl, mix together pork and plenty of black pepper. Set aside for 30 minutes.

In a wok or frying pan, heat oil, add garlic and cook, stirring occasionally, for 2-3 minutes, then stir in pork.

Stir briefly until pork changes colour. Stir in mixed vegetables, then fish sauce, sugar and 125 ml (4 fl oz/½ cup) water. Stir for 3-4 minutes until mange tout (snow peas) are bright green and vegetables still crisp. Stir in spring onions (scallions).

Serves 4.

—PORK WITH SPRING ONIONS—

625 ml (20 fl oz/2½ cups) coconut milk
450 g (1 lb) lean pork, cut into 2.5 cm (1 in) cubes
1 tablespoon fish sauce
½ teaspoon crushed palm sugar
100 g (3½ oz/1 cup) skinned peanuts
3 fresh red chillies, seeded and chopped
3 cm (1¼ in) piece galangal, chopped
4 cloves garlic
1 stalk lemon grass, chopped
4 tablespoons coconut cream, see page 11
8 spring onions (scallions), chopped
1 kg (2 lb) young spinach leaves
warmed coconut cream, see page 11, and dry-roasted
    peanuts, to serve

In a wok, heat coconut milk just to simmering point, adjust heat so liquid barely moves. Add pork and cook for about 25 minutes until very tender. Meanwhile, using a small blender or food processor, mix fish sauce, sugar, peanuts, chillies, galangal, garlic and lemon grass to a paste. In another wok, or a frying pan, heat coconut cream until oil separates. Add spring onions (scallions) and peanut paste and cook, stirring frequently, for 2-3 minutes.

Stir in milk from pork and boil until lightly thickened. Pour over pork, stir and cook for 5 minutes more. Rinse spinach leaves, then pack into a saucepan with just water left on them. Gently cook for about 3 minutes until just beginning to wilt. Arrange on a warmed serving plate. Spoon pork and sauce onto centre. Trickle over coconut cream and scatter over dry-roasted peanuts.

Serves 4-6.

PORK & PRAWN NOODLES

200 g (7 oz) bean thread noodles
6 dried Chinese black mushrooms
2 tablespoons vegetable oil
350 g (12 oz) lean pork, very finely chopped
115 g (4 oz) cooked peeled large prawns
3 red shallots, finely chopped
4 spring onions (scallions), including some green,
   sliced
3 slim inner celery stalks, thinly sliced
55 g (2 oz) dried shrimps
2 tablespoons fish sauce
5 tablespoons lime juice
1½ teaspoons crushed palm sugar
2 fresh red chillies, seeded and chopped
15 g (½ oz) coriander leaves, chopped
whole cooked prawns and coriander, to garnish

Soak noodles in cold water for 15 minutes. Soak mushrooms in water for 30 minutes. Drain and chop. In a wok, heat oil, add pork and stir-fry for 2-3 minutes until cooked through. Using a slotted spoon, transfer to absorbent kitchen paper. Add noodles to a saucepan of boiling water and boil for 5 minutes. Drain well and set aside.

Cut each prawn into 3 and place in a bowl. Add shallots, spring onions (scallions), celery, mushrooms, noodles, pork and dried shrimps; toss together. In a small bowl, mix together fish sauce, lime juice and sugar. Pour into bowl, add coriander leaves and toss ingredients together. Serve garnished with whole prawns and coriander sprigs.

Serves 4.

CRISPY NOODLES

175 g (6 oz) rice vermicelli
6 pieces dried Chinese black mushrooms
115 g (4 oz) lean pork
115 g (4 oz) chicken breast
vegetable oil for deep frying
2 eggs
4 cloves garlic, finely chopped
3 shallots, thinly sliced
1 fresh red chilli, seeded and sliced
1 fresh green chilli, seeded and sliced
6 tablespoons lime juice
1 tablespoon fish sauce
1 tablespoon crushed palm sugar
45 g (1½ oz) cooked peeled shrimps
115 g (4 oz) beansprouts
3 spring onions (scallions), thickly sliced

Soak vermicelli in water for 20 minutes, then drain and set aside. Soak mushrooms in water for 20 minutes, then drain, chop and set aside. Cut pork and chicken into 2.5 cm (1 in) strips or small dice. Set aside.

For garnish, heat 2 teaspoons oil in a wok. In a small bowl, beat eggs with 2 tablespoons water, then drip small amounts in batches in tear shapes onto wok. Cook for 1½-2 minutes until set. Remove using a fish slice or thin spatula. Set aside.

Add more oil to wok until there is sufficient for deep frying. Heat to 190C (375F). Add vermicelli in batches and fry until puffed, light golden brown and crisp. Transfer to absorbent kitchen paper. Set aside.

Pour off oil leaving 3 tablespoons. Add garlic and shallots and cook, stirring occasionally, until lightly browned. Add pork, stir-fry for 1 minute, then mix in chicken and stir for 2 minutes. Stir in chillies, mushrooms, lime juice, fish sauce and sugar.

Bubble until liquid becomes very lightly syrupy. Add shrimps, beansprouts and noodles, tossing to coat with sauce without breaking up noodles. Serve with spring onions (scallions) scattered over and garnished with egg 'tears'.

Serves 4.

– CRAB & AUBERGINE NOODLES –

225 g (8 oz) brown and white crab meat
175 g (6 oz) dried egg thread noodles
3 tablespoons vegetable oil
1 aubergine (eggplant), about 225 g (8 oz), cut into
    about 5 x 0.5 cm (2 x ¼ in) strips
2 cloves garlic, very finely chopped
1 cm (½ in) slice galangal, finely chopped
1 fresh green chilli, seeded and finely chopped
6 spring onions (scallions), sliced
1 tablespoon fish sauce
2 teaspoons lime juice
1½ tablespoons chopped coriander leaves

In a bowl, well mash brown crab meat. Roughly mash white meat. Set aside.

Add noodles to a saucepan of boiling salted water and cook for about 4 minutes until just tender. Drain well. Meanwhile, in a wok, heat 2 tablespoons oil, add aubergine (eggplant) and stir-fry for about 5 minutes until evenly well coloured. Using a slotted spoon, transfer to absorbent kitchen paper; set aside.

Add remaining oil to wok, heat, then one by one stir in garlic, galangal, chilli, finally spring onions (scallions). Add noodles, toss together for 1 minute, then toss in crab meats and aubergine (eggplant). Sprinkle over fish sauce, lime juice and coriander, and toss to mix. Garnish with coriander sprig.

Serves 3.

–CHICKEN & MUSHROOM RICE–

175 g (6 oz/¾ cup) long-grain white rice
2 tablespoons vegetable oil
1 small onion, finely chopped
2 cloves garlic, finely chopped
2 fresh red chillies, seeded and cut into slivers
225 g (8 oz) chicken breast meat, finely chopped
85 g (3 oz) bamboo shoots, chopped or cut into
  matchstick strips
8 pieces dried Chinese black mushrooms, soaked for 30
  minutes, drained and chopped
2 tablespoons dried shrimps
1 tablespoon fish sauce
about 25 Thai holy basil leaves
Thai holy basil sprig, to garnish

Cook rice, see page 12. In a wok, heat oil, add onion and garlic and cook, stirring occasionally, until golden. Add chillies and chicken and stir-fry for 2 minutes.

Stir in bamboo shoots, mushrooms, dried shrimps and fish sauce. Continue to stir for 2 minutes, then stir in rice and basil. Serve garnished with basil sprig.

Serves 4.

THAI FRIED RICE

175 g (6 oz/¾ cup) long-grain white rice
115 g (4 oz) long beans, or French beans, cut into
    2.5 cm (1 in) lengths
3 tablespoons vegetable oil
2 onions, finely chopped
3 cloves garlic, crushed
85 g (3 oz) lean pork, very finely chopped
85 g (3 oz) chicken breast meat, very finely chopped
2 eggs, beaten
2 tablespoons Nam Prik, see page 16
1 tablespoon fish sauce
85 g (3 oz) cooked peeled prawns
coriander leaves, sliced spring onions (scallions) and
    lime wedges, to garnish

Cook rice, see page 12. Add beans to a sauce-pan of boiling water and cook for 2 minutes. Drain and refresh under cold running water. Drain well. In a wok, heat oil, add onions and garlic and cook, stirring occasionally, until softened. Stir in pork and chicken and stir-fry for 1 minute. Push to side of wok.

Pour eggs into centre of wok, leave until just beginning to set, then stir in pork mixture followed by nam prik, fish sauce and rice. Stir for 1-2 minutes, then add beans and prawns. Serve garnished with coriander leaves, spring onions (scallions) and lime wedges.

Serves 4.

──STIR-FRIED MANGE TOUT──

2 tablespoons vegetable oil
3 cloves garlic, finely chopped
115 g (4 oz) lean pork, very finely chopped
450 g (1 lb) mange tout (snow peas)
½ teaspoon crushed palm sugar
1 tablespoon fish sauce
55 g (2 oz) cooked peeled prawns, chopped
freshly ground black pepper

In a wok, heat oil over a medium heat, add garlic and fry until lightly coloured. Add pork and stir-fry for 2-3 minutes.

Add mange tout (snow peas) and stir-fry for about 3 minutes until cooked but still crisp.

Stir in sugar, fish sauce, prawns and black pepper. Heat briefly and serve.

Serves 4-6.

STUFFED AUBERGINES

2 aubergines (eggplants), each about 225 g (8 oz)
2 cloves garlic, finely chopped
2 stalks lemon grass, chopped
2 tablespoons vegetable oil
1 small onion, finely chopped
175 g (6 oz) chicken breast meat, finely chopped
2 teaspoons fish sauce
25 Thai holy basil leaves
freshly ground black pepper
Thai holy basil leaves, to garnish

Preheat grill. Place aubergines (eggplants) under grill and cook, turning as necessary, for about 20 minutes until evenly charred.

Meanwhile, using a pestle and mortar, pound together garlic and lemon grass; set aside. Heat oil in a wok, add onion and cook, stirring occasionally, until lightly browned. Stir in garlic mixture, cook for 1-2 minutes, then add chicken. Stir-fry for 2 minutes. Stir in fish sauce, basil leaves and plenty of black pepper.

Using a sharp knife, slice each charred aubergine (eggplant) in half lengthwise. Using a teaspoon, carefully scoop aubergine (eggplant) flesh into a bowl; keep skins warm. Using kitchen scissors, chop flesh. Add to wok and stir ingredients together for about 1 minute. Place aubergine (eggplant) skins on a large warmed plate and divide chicken mixture between them. Garnish with basil leaves.

Serves 4.

SPICED CABBAGE

14 black peppercorns
2 tablespoons coconut cream, see page 11
2 shallots, chopped
115 g (4 oz) lean pork, very finely chopped
about 450 g (1 lb) white cabbage, finely sliced
315 ml (10 fl oz/1¼ cups) coconut milk
1 tablespoon fish sauce
1 fresh red chilli, seeded and very finely chopped

In a wok, heat peppercorns for about 3 minutes until aroma changes. Stir in coconut cream, heat for 2-3 minutes, then stir in shallots.

Stir-fry for a further 2-3 minutes, then stir in pork and cabbage. Cook, stirring occasionally, for 3 minutes, then add coconut milk and bring just to the boil. Cover and simmer for 5 minutes.

Uncover and cook for about 10 minutes until cabbage is tender but retains some bite. Stir in fish sauce. Serve sprinkled with chilli.

Serves 4-5.

——VEGETABLES WITH SAUCE——

1 aubergine (eggplant), about 225 g (8 oz)
115 g (4 oz) long beans or green beans
85 g (3 oz) cauliflower flowerets
500 ml (16 fl oz/2 cups) coconut milk
2 red shallots, chopped
2 cloves garlic, chopped
4 coriander roots, chopped
2 dried red chillies, seeded and chopped
1 stalk lemon grass, chopped
3 cm (1¼ in) piece galangal, chopped
grated peel 1 kaffir lime
4 tablespoons coconut cream, see page 11
1½ tablespoons ground roasted peanuts
3 tablespoons tamarind water, see page 13
1 tablespoon fish sauce
2 teaspoons crushed palm sugar

Cut aubergine (eggplant) into 4 cm (1½ in) cubes; cut beans into 5 cm (2 in) lengths. Put aubergine (eggplant), beans and cauliflower into a saucepan, add coconut milk and bring to the boil. Cover and simmer for 10 minutes until vegetables are tender. Remove from heat, uncover and set aside. Using a pestle and mortar or small blender, pound or mix together shallots, garlic, coriander roots, chillies, lemon grass, galangal and lime peel.

Mix in 4 tablespoons liquid from the vegetables. Place in a small, heavy frying pan, stir in coconut cream and heat, stirring, until oil is released and paste is thick. Stir into vegetables with peanuts, tamarind water, fish sauce and sugar. Heat through gently for about 1 minute.

Serves 6.

MUSHROOMS & BEANSPROUTS

2 tablespoons vegetable oil
2 fresh red chillies, seeded and thinly sliced
2 cloves garlic, chopped
225 g (8 oz) shiitake mushrooms, sliced
115 g (4 oz) beansprouts
115 g (4 oz) cooked peeled prawns
2 tablespoons lime juice
2 red shallots, sliced into rings
1 tablespoon fish sauce
½ teaspoon crushed palm sugar
1 tablespoon ground browned rice, see page 13
6 coriander sprigs, stalks and leaves finely chopped
10 Thai mint leaves, shredded
Thai mint leaves, to garnish

In a wok, heat oil, add chillies and garlic and cook, stirring occasionally, for 2-3 minutes. Add mushrooms and stir-fry for 2-3 minutes.

Add beansprouts and prawns, stir-fry for 1 minute, then stir in lime juice, shallots, fish sauce and sugar. When hot, remove from heat and stir in rice, coriander and mint. Serve garnished with mint leaves.

Serves 4.

CHICKEN & WATERCRESS SALAD

2 cloves garlic, finely chopped
3 cm (1¼ in) piece galangal, finely chopped
1 tablespoon fish sauce
3 tablespoons lime juice
1 teaspoon crushed palm sugar
2 tablespoons peanut oil
225 g (8 oz) chicken breast meat, finely chopped
about 25 dried shrimps
1 bunch watercress, about 115 g (4 oz), coarse stalks
   removed
3 tablespoons chopped dry-roasted peanuts
2 fresh red chillies, seeded and cut into fine strips

Using a pestle and mortar, pound together garlic and galangal. Mix in fish sauce, lime juice and sugar; set aside. In wok, heat oil, add chicken and stir-fry for about 3 minutes until cooked through. Using a slotted spoon, transfer to absorbent kitchen paper to drain. Put into a serving bowl and set aside.

Chop half dried shrimps and add to bowl. Mix in watercress, peanuts and half of chillies. Pour over garlic mixture and toss to mix. Sprinkle with remaining chillies and shrimps.

Serves 3-4.

—— CHICKEN & MINT SALAD ——

1 stalk lemon grass, finely chopped
2-3 fresh red chillies, seeded and finely chopped
3 tablespoons lime juice
1 tablespoon crushed palm sugar
1½ tablespoons vegetable oil
450 g (1 lb) skinless chicken breast meat, very finely
   chopped
15 Thai mint leaves, shredded
lettuce leaves, to serve
mint sprig, to garnish

In a bowl, mix together lemon grass, chillies,
lime juice, fish sauce and sugar, set aside.

In a wok, heat oil, stir in chicken and cook
over a fairly high heat, stirring, for about 1½
minutes until cooked through. Using a slotted spoon, quickly transfer to absorbent
kitchen paper to drain, then add to bowl.

Add mint and toss lightly. Serve on a bed of
lettuce leaves, garnished with mint sprig.

Serves 4.

BEAN SALAD

2 tablespoons lime juice
2 tablespoons fish sauce
½ teaspoon crushed palm sugar
1½ tablespoons Nam Prik, see page 16
2 tablespoons ground roasted peanuts
2 tablespoons vegetable oil
3 cloves garlic, chopped
3 shallots, thinly sliced
¼ dried red chilli, seeded and finely chopped
2 tablespoons coconut cream, see page 11
225 g (8 oz) French beans, very thinly sliced

In a small bowl, mix together lime juice, fish sauce, sugar, nam prik, peanuts and 2 tablespoons water; set aside. In a small saucepan, heat oil, add garlic and shallots and cook, stirring occasionally, until beginning to brown. Stir in chilli and cook until garlic and shallots are browned. Using a slotted spoon, transfer to absorbent kitchen paper; set aside.

In a small saucepan over a low heat, warm coconut cream, stirring occasionally. Bring a saucepan of water to the boil, add beans, return to the boil and cook for about 30 seconds. Drain and refresh under cold running water. Drain well. Transfer to a serving bowl and toss with shallot mixture and contents of small bowl. Spoon over warm coconut cream.

Serves 3-4.

— HOT BAMBOO SHOOT SALAD —

1 tablespoon fish sauce
2 tablespoons tamarind water, see page 13
½ teaspoon crushed palm sugar
1 clove garlic, finely chopped
1 small fresh red chilli, seeded and finely chopped
175 g (6 oz) bamboo shoots, cut into fine strips
1 tablespoon coarsely ground browned rice,
    see page 13
2 spring onions (scallions), including some green part,
    sliced
coriander leaves, to garnish

In a saucepan, heat fish sauce, tamarind water, sugar, garlic, chilli and 2 tablespoons water to the boil. Stir in bamboo shoots and heat for 1-2 minutes.

Stir in rice, then turn into a warmed dish, scatter over spring onion (scallion) and garnish with coriander leaves.

Serves 2-3.

—MANGO WITH STICKY RICE—

225 g (8 oz/1¼ cups) sticky rice, soaked overnight in
   cold water
250 ml (8 fl oz/1 cup) coconut milk
pinch salt
2-4 tablespoons sugar, to taste
2 large ripe mangoes, peeled and halved
3 tablespoons coconut cream, see page 11
mint leaves to decorate

Drain and rinse rice thoroughly. Place in a
steaming basket lined with a double thickness
of muslin. Steam over simmering water for 30
minutes. Remove from heat.

In a bowl, stir together coconut milk, salt and
sugar to taste until sugar has dissolved. Stir in
warm rice. Set aside for 30 minutes.

Thinly slice mangoes by cutting lengthwise
through flesh to the stone. Discard the
stones. Spoon rice into a mound in centre
of serving plates and arrange mango slices
around. Pour coconut cream over rice.
Decorate with mint leaves.

Serves 4.

COCONUT PANCAKES

115 g (4 oz/⅔ cup) rice flour
85 g (3 oz/⅓ cup) caster sugar
pinch salt
85 g (3 oz/1 cup) desiccated coconut
2 eggs, beaten
625 ml (20 fl oz/2½ cups) coconut milk
green and red food colouring, if desired
vegetable oil for frying
mandarin segments, to serve, if desired

In a bowl, stir together rice flour, sugar, salt and coconut.

Form a well in centre, add egg, then gradually draw in flour, slowly pouring in coconut milk at same time, to make a smooth batter. If desired, divide batter evenly between 3 bowls. Stir green food colouring into one bowl to colour batter pale green; colour another batch pink and leave remaining batch plain. Heat a 15 cm (6 in) crêpe or omelette pan over a moderate heat, swirl around a little oil, then pour off excess. Stir batter well, then add 2-3 spoonfuls to pan.

Rotate to cover base, then cook over moderate heat for about 4 minutes until lightly browned underneath and quite firmly set. Carefully turn over and cook briefly on other side. Transfer to a warmed plate and keep warm while cooking remaining batter. Serve rolled up with mandarin segments, if liked.

Makes about 10.

Note: The mixture is quite delicate and the first few pancakes may be troublesome.

LYCHEES & COCONUT CUSTARD

3 egg yolks
3-4 tablespoons caster sugar
200 ml (7 fl oz/scant 1 cup) coconut milk
85 ml (3 fl oz/⅓ cup) coconut cream, see page 11
about 1 tablespoon triple distilled rose water
red food colouring
about 16 fresh lychees, peeled, halved and stones
    removed
rose petals, to decorate

In a bowl, whisk together egg yolks and sugar.

In a medium, preferably non-stick, saucepan, heat coconut milk to just below boiling point, then slowly stir into bowl. Return to pan and cook very gently, stirring with a wooden spoon, until custard coats the back of the spoon.

Remove from heat and stir in coconut cream, rose water to taste and sufficient red food colouring to colour pale pink. Leave until cold, stirring occasionally. Spoon a thin layer of rose-flavoured custard into 4 small serving bowls. Arrange lychees on custard. Decorate with rose petals. Serve remaining custard separately to pour over lychees.

Serves 4.

GOLDEN THREADS

5 egg yolks
1 teaspoon egg white
450 g (1 lb/2 cups) sugar
few drops jasmine essence

Strain egg yolks through muslin into a small bowl. Beat lightly with egg white. In a saucepan, gently heat sugar, jasmine essence and 250 ml (8 fl oz/1 cup) water, stirring until sugar dissolves, then boil until thickened slightly. Adjust heat so syrup is hot but not moving.

Spoon a small amount of egg yolk into a piping bag fitted with a very fine nozzle or a cone of greaseproof paper with very small hole in pointed end. Using a circular movement, carefully dribble a trail into syrup, making swirls about 4-5 cm (1½-2 in) in diameter with a small hole in centre. Make a few at a time, cooking each briefly until set.

Using a skewer inserted in hole in centre of spiral, transfer each nest to a plate. Continue making similar nests with remaining egg yolks. When nests are cool, arrange on a serving plate.

Serves 4.

INDEX